A Mother Who Prayed

1 Samuel 1:1–28 for children

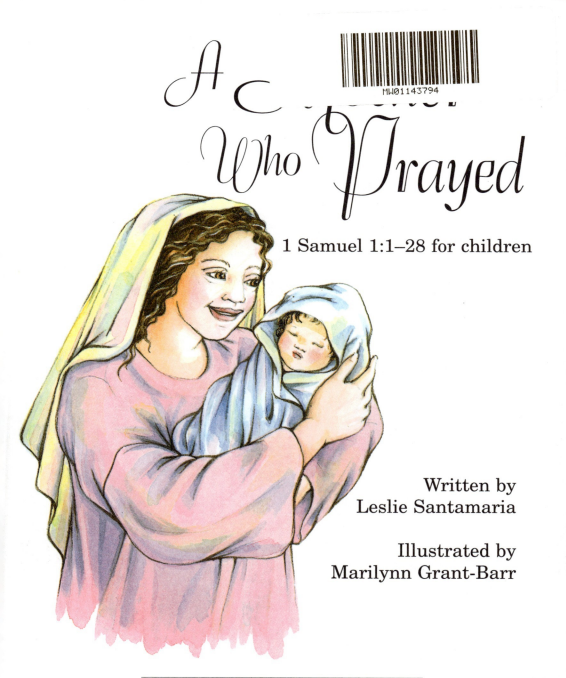

Written by
Leslie Santamaria

Illustrated by
Marilynn Grant-Barr

CONCORDIA PUBLISHING HOUSE · SAINT LOUIS

Hannah was one of Elkanah's wives.
She had no children and felt disgrace.
His other wife had many babes
Who all resembled Elkanah's face.

Elkanah went to the temple
To worship and offer sacrifice.
Then meat he gave each wife
and child,
But on Hannah's plate he
served twice.

Year after year the other wife
Would tease poor Hannah and make her cry.
Because the Lord had closed her womb,
Hannah's sinking heart ached deep inside.

Elkanah loved his wife so much.
Oft he asked, "Why weep as you do?
Why are you so downhearted, my wife?
Am *I* not worth *ten* sons to you?"

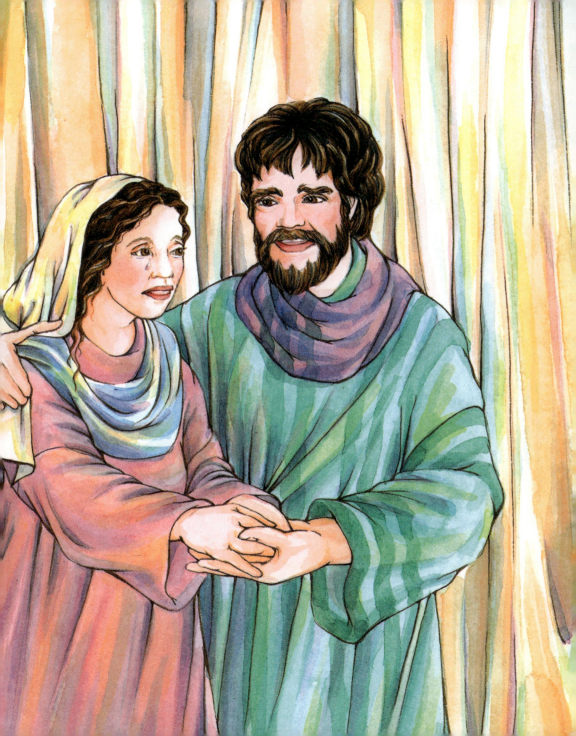

One day on a temple visit,
Hannah stood as she finished her meal.
Nearby Priest Eli saw her pray
And cry out to the Lord with such zeal.

"Almighty, please remember me.
With a son, now please bless Your servant.
I vow to give him back to You
Because to me he is merely lent."

Hannah's lips moved without a sound.
Priest Eli thought that something was wrong.
"No," said Hannah, "I'm just praying
For a joy I have wanted so long."

Eli answered, "Now go in peace.
May our God bestow what you
    have asked."
With hope she left and even ate.
Hannah's face was no longer
    downcast.

Early next day at the temple,
As the sun did break through the dark,
The man and wife worshiped their Lord first,
And toward home they then did embark.

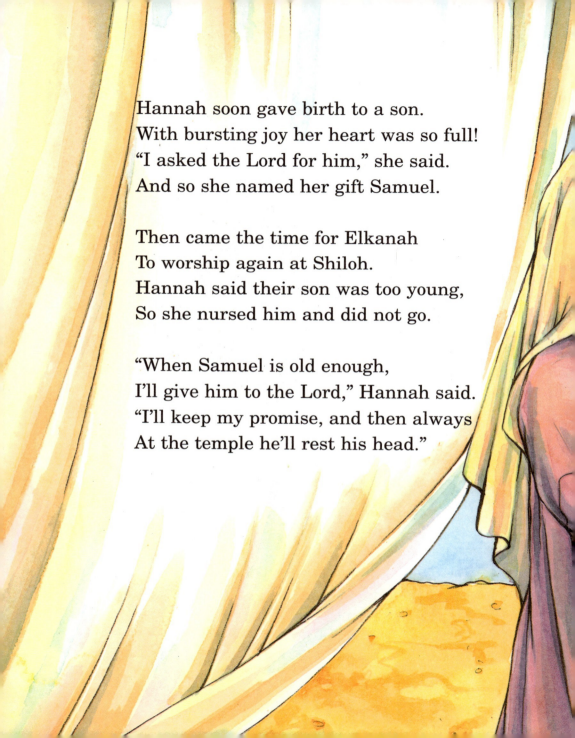

Hannah soon gave birth to a son.
With bursting joy her heart was so full!
"I asked the Lord for him," she said.
And so she named her gift Samuel.

Then came the time for Elkanah
To worship again at Shiloh.
Hannah said their son was too young,
So she nursed him and did not go.

"When Samuel is old enough,
I'll give him to the Lord," Hannah said.
"I'll keep my promise, and then always
At the temple he'll rest his head."

Elkanah agreed with his wife,
For Hannah's vow had to be
   fulfilled.
With a bull, some flour,
   and wine,
She completed what her God
   had willed.

She took her son to the temple
When Samuel was just a young boy.
To Eli she said, "I'm the one
You saw praying to God for this joy.

"I prayed for this child,"
   said Hannah.
And great thankfulness
   glowed on her face.
"Now I give him back
   to my God.
He will worship and learn
   in this place."

Thank You, God, for hearing *our* prayers.
Your wise answers are perfect for us.
Help *us* to pray like Hannah did:
Without ceasing and with heartfelt trust.

Dear Parents:

Take a moment to read the prayer Hannah prays to God *after* she has given Samuel to the Lord. This prayer is found in 1 Samuel 2:1–10. It is a prayer of praise and thanksgiving. Her joy is not in her son, but in God who answered her prayer.

God hears the prayers of all Christians and answers them in His own way and at His own time. In prayer, we come to God as His children, as brothers and sisters of Christ who redeemed us. Through Christ we can boldly approach God in prayer, knowing that He will listen and answer our prayers in ways He knows are best for us.

Let your child see and hear you pray. Involve your child in prayers, whether using memorized prayers as part of a ritual such as bedtime or praying spontaneous prayers for specific situations. Make talking with Jesus as comfortable and natural as your family conversations. And remember the words of 1 Thessalonians 5:16–18 (NIV): *Be joyful always; pray continuously; give thanks in all circumstances, for this is God's will for you in Christ Jesus.*

The Editor